S0-BDL-819

The Unicorn Poop
JOKE BOOK

ARCTURUS

ARCTURUS

This edition published in 2020 by Arcturus Publishing Limited
26/27 Bickels Yard, 151–153 Bermondsey Street,
London SE1 3HA

Copyright © Arcturus Holdings Limited

All rights reserved. No part of this publication may be reproduced,
stored in a retrieval system, or transmitted, in any form or by
any means, electronic, mechanical, photocopying, recording, or
otherwise, without prior written permission in accordance with the
provisions of the Copyright Act 1956 (as amended). Any person or
persons who do any unauthorized act in relation to this publication
may be liable to criminal prosecution and civil claims for damages.

Author: Jack B. Quick
Illustrator: Gareth Conway
Designer: Trudi Webb
Editor: Violet Peto
Art Director: Jessica Holliland
Managing Editor: Joe Harris

ISBN: 978-1-83857-593-9
CH007791NT
Supplier 29, Date 0320, Print run 9492

Printed in China

3

What do you call a unicorn with no horn?

Completely pointless!

What's big, ugly, and blue?

A monster holding its breath!

5

What do you call a baby unicorn?

A uni-kernel!

What do you call it when the queen goes to the bathroom?

A royal flush!

What do
snowmen sing
to Santa Claus?

"Freeze a jolly
good fellow!"

What did the
Easter bunny say
to the carrot?

"It's been nice
gnawing you!"

Do you like the jokes in this book?

No, they're too uni-corny!

What do you call a sprite with a twisted ankle?

A hoblin' goblin!

What do you call a magical dog?

A labra-cadabra-dor!

What do you call a witch at the beach?

A sand witch!

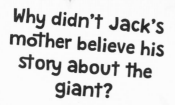

Why didn't Jack's mother believe his story about the giant?

He was always telling tall tales!

Why did the baker stop making donuts?

She was bored of the hole business!

FLOUR

14

Did you hear about the magician who could make himself invisible?

He wasn't much to look at!

What is a queen's most treasured item of clothing?

Her reign-coat!

What's a ghost's top party game?

Hide and shriek!

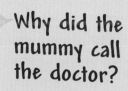

Why did the mummy call the doctor?

Because it was coffin!

Why can you always hear mumbling outside Jack's house?

Because Jack and the beans talk!

What did the witch do when she got on stage?

She gave a screech!

Why did Little Miss Muffet need a map?

Because she'd lost her whey!

Why is Snow White kind to all seven dwarfs?

Because she's the fairest of them all!

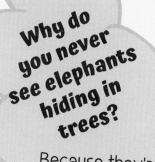

Why do you never see elephants hiding in trees?

Because they're so good at it!

What does a zombie read first in the newspaper?

Its horrorscope!

What was Camelot famous for?

Its knight life!

Knock, knock!
Who's there?
Jacqueline.
Jacqueline who?

Jacqueline Hyde,
watch out!

What dessert do swamp monsters like best?

Key slime pie!

Where did King Arthur's men get their training?

Knight school!

What do you call it when a queen passes wind?

Noble gas!

How much did Santa pay for his sleigh?

Nothing, it was on the house!

27

What did the
ocean say to
the mermaid?

Nothing. It
just waved!

Where do you
find giant
snails?

On a giant's
fingers!

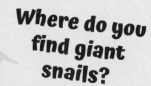

Where do mermaids sleep?

On a waterbed!

When are you allowed to take bubblegum to school?

On chews-day!

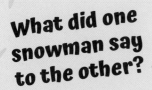

What did one snowman say to the other?

"Can you smell carrots?"

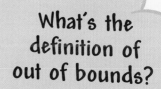

What's the definition of out of bounds?

An exhausted kangaroo!

What's the difference between ice cream and milk chocolate?

Anyone can scream, but no one can milk chocolate!

What did the pirate say on his 80th birthday?

Aye, matey!

What do you call a deer that can use all four hooves?

Bambidextrous!

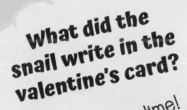

What did the snail write in the valentine's card?

Be my valen-slime!

Why did the dragon breathe on the map of the Earth?

Because he wanted to set the world on fire!

Why was the firefly unhappy?

Because her children weren't so bright!

Why was Cinderella no good at sports?

Because her coach was a pumpkin!

What do you shout when santa takes the roll call?

Present!

How many skunks does is take to make a big stink?

Quite a phew!

Why did the dragon join the gym?

It wanted to burn more calories!

Which owl robbed the rich to give to the poor?

Robin Hoot!

How do you get a baby alien to sleep?

Rocket!

Who delivers presents to pets?

Santa Claws!

Who dresses in red and white, and is a danger in the water?

Santa Jaws!

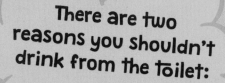

There are two reasons you shouldn't drink from the toilet:

Number one and number two!

Why was Cinderella thrown off the sports team?

She kept running away from the ball!

Why did
Rapunzel go
wild at parties?

She liked to
let her hair
down!

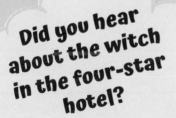

Did you hear
about the witch
in the four-star
hotel?

She ordered
broom service!

What does Medusa do on a bad hair day?

She pays a visit to the snake charmer!

What does a mermaid do on her birthday?

She shellebrates!

42

Did you hear about the tooth fairy who became a judge?

She wanted the tooth, the whole tooth, and nothing but the tooth!

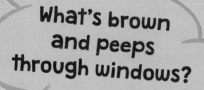

What's brown and peeps through windows?

A poop on stilts!

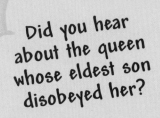

Did you hear about the queen whose eldest son disobeyed her?

She was having a bad heir day!

What food do unicorns like best?

Uni-corncobs!

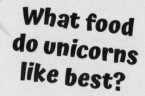

44

When is the best time to buy Easter chicks?

When they are going cheep!

Who's the worst player on the ghoul soccer team?

The grim keeper!

What music was popular with Egyptian mummies?

Wrap music!

Did you hear about the witches who were identical twins?

You couldn't tell which witch was which!

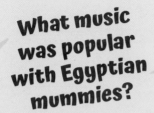

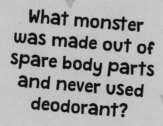

What monster was made out of spare body parts and never used deodorant?

Stankenstein!

What do you call a fairy who never takes baths?

Stinkerbell!

What do you call a wizard who keeps falling over?

Stumbledore!

What's a monster's top party game?

Swallow my leader!

49

Have you seen the new movie, Constipated?

It hasn't come out yet!

How do monsters like their eggs?

Terror-fried!

What did Robin Hood say when he nearly got shot at the archery contest?

That was an arrow escape!

Did you hear about the bald unicorn?

She had the mane part missing!

Did you hear about the man who ate 24 cans of alphabet soup?

He has trouble with his vowels!

What was the first animal in space?

The cow that jumped over the moon!

Where do mummies go to the beach?

The Dead Sea!

Who granted the fish's wish?

The fairy cod mother!

Who saves drowning spooks at the seaside?

The ghostguard!

What do magical creatures eat for breakfast?

Unicorn-flakes!

What tastes delicious and knows karate?

The ninjabread man!

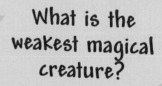

What is the weakest magical creature?

The puny-corn!

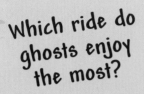

Which ride do ghosts enjoy the most?

The roller ghoster!

What's brown, furry, and has twelve legs?

The three bears!

57

What do birds do on Halloween?

They go trick-or-tweeting!

What do narwhals do in their spare time?

They just chill!

Why should you never tell a burrito a secret?

They might spill the beans!

Why did soldiers fire arrows from the castle?

They were trying to get their point across!

Why can you trust mummies with your secrets?

They're good at keeping things under wraps!

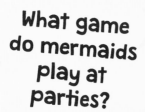

What game do mermaids play at parties?

Tide-and-seek!

What do dragons call knights?

Canned food!

Why did the mermaid cross the ocean?

To get to the other tide!

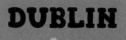

How can you tell
that a leprechaun
is enjoying herself?

She's Dublin over
with laughter!

What did
one toilet
say to the
other?

You look
flushed!

What's the best way to greet a werewolf?

Howl do you do?

Knock, knock!
Who's there?
Donut!
Donut who?

Donut ask, it's a secret!

What did the chef write in her valentine's card?

I love you from my head tomatoes!

Sugar is sweet, lemons are tart ...

I love you more than a unicorn fart!

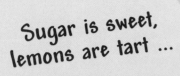

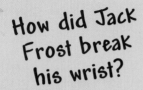

How did Jack Frost break his wrist?

He fell off his icicle!

How did the skeleton know he had found true love?

He felt it in his bones!

Did you hear about the unicorn whose tail dropped off?

She went to the retail store!

What's brown and sticky?

A stick!

What do mermaids post on social media?

Shellfies!

What was the first thing said by the inventor of the stink bomb?

You reek, ugh!

Which knight was King Arthur's best lookout?

Sir Veillance!

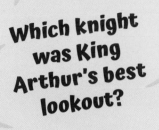

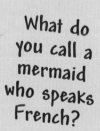

What do you call a mermaid who speaks French?

So-fish-ticated!

Why was the genie grumpy when he came out of his lamp?

Someone had rubbed him up the wrong way!

Where can you weigh a pie?

Somewhere over the rainbow!

What did
the skeleton
order at the
restaurant?

Spare ribs!

How do little
witches listen to
bedtime stories?

Spellbound!

What is the sweetest, squishiest, scariest day of the year?

Marshmalloween!

MEDIUM

What do you call a troll of average size?

Medi-ogre!

Why should you be especially afraid of a vampire dog?

It's bite is worse than its bark!

What was Robin's mother called?

Motherhood!

73

What should you say to Simba if he's walking too slowly?

Mufasa!

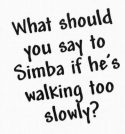

Why are dinosaurs no longer around?

Because their eggs stink!

What do you call a deer with no eyes?

No eye deer!

How do vampires get clean?

In a blood bath!

Hi, you're through to the Diarrhoea Hotline ... can you hold, please?

Why do witches ride on broomsticks?

Because vacuums suck!

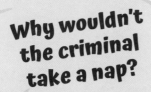

Why wouldn't the criminal take a nap?

He was resisting a rest!

SWAG

What gift did the smelly bee receive from its friends?

Bee-oderant!

Which nursery rhyme character talks too much?

Blah blah black sheep!

What kind of music do mermaids like?

Bubble rap!

How can you send a letter to the Easter bunny?

By hare mail!

What does a nut say when it sneezes?

Cashew!

Why did the baker have smelly hands?

Because she kneaded a poop!

How does the Easter bunny stay fit?

Eggs-ercise!

What do mermaids read at bedtime?

Ferry tales!

Which monster is good at science?

Frank Einstein!

What does Cinderella wear underwater?

Glass flippers!

What sport do unicorns like the best?

Glitterball!

What can you see flying through the sky on Christmas eve?

A U.F. Ho ho ho!

What do you call a horse with a fake horn?

A uni-con!

Did you hear about the single monster who tried online dating?

She was looking for an edible bachelor!

How did Jack count how many beans his cow was worth?

He used a cow-culator!

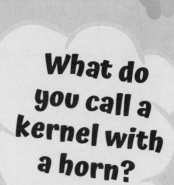

Why did the pie go to the dentist?

It needed a filling!

What do you call a kernel with a horn?

A unique corn!

How did the hunchback of Notre Dame take his sore throat medicine?

He gargoyled it!

Why did the wizard visit the doctor?

He had a dizzy spell!

What happened to the snowman in the spring?

He made a pool of himself!

Why does Peter Pan fly everywhere?

He never, never lands!

Did you hear about the magician who lost his temper on stage?

He pulled his hare out!

Why do monsters go to the disco?

To boogie, man!

What has three horns, five legs, and two tails?

A unicorn with spare parts!

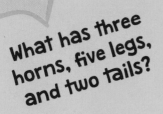

Why did the lion eat the tightrope walker?

He wanted a balanced meal!

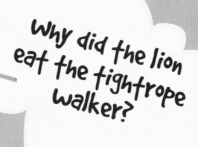

What do you call a ghostly chicken?

A poultry-geist!

WOOOoo..

What do you call a unicorn with three eyes?

A uniiicorn!